Go
the
Distance

Go the Distance

Making Strides Towards Life Goals

BILL CHAMBERS

Toronto, Ontario
2003

Go The Distance
Copyright © 2003 Bill Chambers

All rights reserved. No part of this book may be reproduced in any manner without the express written consent of the publisher, except in the case of brief excerpts in critical reviews and articles. All inquiries should be addressed to:

Bill Chambers
50 Willow Avenue, Toronto Ontario M4E 3K2
E-mail: bill_chambers@canada.com

National Library of Canada Cataloguing in Publication

Chambers, Bill, 1953-
Go the distance : making strides towards life goals / Bill Chambers.

ISBN 0-9732768-0-0

1. Success--Psychological aspects. 2. Marathon running. I. Title.

BF637.S8C395 2003   158.1   C2003-902297-8

Cover / book design:	Karen Petherick,
	Intuitive Design International Ltd.
Illustrations:	Jane Montague
Cover art:	Photodisc © 2003

Printed and bound in Canada.

This publication is designed to provide useful advice in regard to the subject matter contained herein. The ideas and suggestions in this book are not intended to substitute for the personal advice of your trained health professional. You may wish to consult your physician before adopting the suggestions in this book. The author and all parties involved with this publication disclaim any liability arising directly or indirectly from the use of this book.

DEDICATION

To my brother, Tom,
for whom the walls have finally come down....
You will never be forgotten and always loved.

TABLE OF CONTENTS

Foreword XI

Introduction XV

1. Setting Goals 1

2. Setting Out 11

3. Coaching 22

4. Training 36

5. Challenges 49

6. The Race 58

7. The Finish Line 69

8. Beyond the Finish Line 77

    Epilogue 83

    What Are Your Goals 87

    Take A Look At Yourself 89

    Training Log 90

Acknowledgements

Several years ago, I shared my thoughts on using running as a metaphor for achieving success in the workplace with my friend, Patrick Langston. The challenge that I faced was how to put my thoughts on paper. Under Patrick's guidance, I was able to begin this journey. However, like many journeys in life, this one got sidetracked and my project was set aside for a few years. Luckily, I was able to resume the journey when I became aware of another friend's passion for writing. Jane Tremblay expressed a keen interest in my project and I eagerly accepted her offer to help. To gain a better understanding of what I wanted to achieve, Jane began to run. Over the course of the next year she trained and successfully completed her first marathon.

To both Patrick and Jane, many thanks, as this book would never have been completed without your help. To my sons: Wil, who shared his artistic talents in the design of the chapters and Derek, as I watch you pursue your dream of being the best mountain bike racer in the nation, thank you. You have both helped me realize that I, too, can continue to pursue my goals and dreams.

Foreword

There are those events in life that alter one's course forever. It was Father's Day 1972, and I was nineteen, rebellious and seemingly invincible when I suffered a near-fatal motorcycle accident. I was left with permanent loss of vision in my left eye, loss of hearing in my left ear, broken bones that would take multiple surgeries and months of rehabilitation to repair, and many shattered dreams. Any athletic aspirations that I had were gone in that single moment.

During the weeks that followed the accident I enjoyed notoriety and a lot of sympathetic attention. But pity, whether from others or from oneself, is not a great motivator. I knew the time would eventually come when I would have to face reality. A reality in which I would need to determine a new sense of purpose and redefine the goals I had once set for myself. But one thing I was sure of, my first and most important goal was to recover my physical strength.

Prior to my accident I had always enjoyed running – it came naturally to me. I decided that it would be the activity that would help me to become fit again. Little did I realize, however, what a challenge the simple act of putting one foot in front of the other would be. Both my depth perception and sense of balance were compromised; I had to learn how to run all over again. It was disheartening. I would return home after short runs with ankles bloodied from banging together because of the sheer awkwardness of my running motion. I trained harder, ran further, welcoming the support of other runners, and discovered a sense of focus and discipline I had never known. My body began to adapt to its new sense of balance and perception; my strength gradually returned and I began to believe that new goals and new achievements were possible.

Over the next twenty-five years I would run more than one hundred distance races, collecting T-shirts, personal bests, and memories that would last me a lifetime.

Both my accident years ago and a more recent battle with cancer have been life-threatening and life-altering experiences. In each case running gave me the structure and discipline so necessary to regaining my strength and finding a new focus. But each experience was quite different. I was only nineteen when I had my accident and twenty-two when I began running. At that time I did not realize how significant the running would become and the impact it would have in the years ahead. At the time it was just a means of getting in shape. I had no vision of becoming a distance runner or of ever competing; I had no goal other than to get fit.

The cancer was different. I was in my early forties and my running career was well established by then. Once again I had dreams: dreams of becoming a master runner on the world scene. Cancer was not in my plans. I was training for an Ironman at the time and at the peak of fitness, but I began to experience certain physical changes that made me realize something was wrong. The diagnosis I received was unexpected and shocked me. I looked at the doctor and said, "So what are we going to do about this? I have a race to run."

I remember getting into an argument with my first surgeon regarding my treatment. He was trying to tell me that it wasn't going to be quite as simple as I'd hoped. But I told him, "Yes it is, because I have a training schedule to keep." As a result, he was not the one who did the surgery or follow-up treatments, because I needed someone with a more positive attitude.

When I walked into the office of the surgeon who did perform the operation, there, in the corner, was a mountain bike. We hit it off right from that first encounter. I knew he could share my vision and proceed with the optimism I needed. It wasn't that I was being flippant or naïve. I understood the seriousness of my situation. But running had taught me that you don't reach finish lines if you're not willing to start. A lot depends on how you decide to approach difficult situations. They happen for a reason; they make us learn and sometimes we can share what we've learned with others.

There is a purpose to all that happens and a goodness that can come out of it. Beating cancer was my new challenge and once again the running was a catalyst to recovery, the Rocky Mountain Marathon proved that recovery is possible.

In 1998, four months after my radiation treatments ended, I was in Canmore, Alberta, the day of the Rocky Mountain Marathon. When I heard about the race I decided I would run it. What was so rewarding was that I was able to do it at all. Having recently finished radiation treatments, I approached this race in a very different way. I understood where I was physically, mentally and emotionally. It was not going to be a day of running a personal best. This race would be a new starting point from which I would establish new goals.

I saw the outcome as positive. Did I run well? Not particularly. Did I finish the race? Yes I did! That was the accomplishment. I set new boundaries for myself, understanding that it was unlikely that I would ever compete again as a seeded runner. But the reality was that I could still run, still compete with new expectations and new goals in mind.

Will I ever be as fast as I once was? Being fast is not important – stepping up to the starting line is.

Running has developed in me a sense of discipline and strength that has been invaluable in my personal and professional life. It has taught me to be grateful for the journey and take pleasure in each and every race, whether good or bad. It has defined my finish lines as being the start of something new, and has allowed me to discover how deep I can dig inside myself to find the strength to take one more step.

Introduction

The impetus for this book comes from two observations I have made over the past several years, both in my financial career and as a marathon runner.

>**Observation 1:** Many people perceived to be high achievers are runners.

>**Observation 2:** One's ability not only to survive, but also to prosper in the new economy, demands a radical new approach to selling because of increasingly sophisticated clients, changing work paradigms and intensified competition.

What is the correlation between running and personal performance?

I began to look at the similarities from the perspective of the mutual funds industry where astronomical sales in 1993 were subjected to a heavy reality check in 1994. Having successfully completed a number of races, I realized that the principles upon which successful marathon running are based have a direct application to achieving goals in one's personal life and career, and specifically in the sales environment. Those principles are goal-setting, training, maintaining discipline and focus, and the ability to adapt to an ever-changing environment.

Perhaps runners are more likely to achieve their goals

because they embrace the marathoner's strategy and apply it to all other aspects of their lives. Although not all of us aspire to become marathoners, each of us can benefit from understanding the runner's formula for achieving success.

This book has been designed using the same approach a runner takes to running a marathon. The chapters are laid out in the order that a runner plans his strategies to become a marathoner. As you read each chapter, compare how you are achieving your goals – both in your personal and professional life – to those of the runner. Keep a notebook handy so you can begin to log your thoughts, plans and strategies that will keep you on the road to success. Just remember, it's never to late to begin training for something new.

Enjoy the journey!

How Long Is A Marathon?

Most people don't know how long a marathon is. When you tell people you've run a marathon, or are going to run one, they often ask "And how many miles is that?" Your immediate response is the obvious, "Twenty-six." But that's just part of the answer. The truth is that a marathon is far more.

As measured, a marathon is only 26.1 miles, but in order to run it, you cover a much greater distance. For a first time marathoner, it may take more than 1000 miles to get to the finish line. For an elite athlete, it may be over a hundred miles a week. All that training culminates in a twenty-six mile endurance test and a few hundred yards of glory. In our personal and professional lives, the outcomes we experience represent only a fraction of the time, energy and heart we put into the training, the preparation, the learning, the growing. Results are only the tip of the iceberg ... the final test.

But always, it is the journey that precedes the race that really matters!

CHAPTER ONE

Setting Goals

"A man's reach should exceed his grasp,
or what's a Heaven for?"...
- Robert Browning, 19th century poet

What possesses apparently normal people to become marathon runners?

Running is a sport, or as some choose to call it, an obsession, that finds you out at 5:30 a.m. in a cold drizzle, pushing your body constantly to make it stronger and more efficient, and, if all goes well, stumbling across the finish line in a state of delirium and exhaustion, euphemistically referred to as a "runner's high."

Every year, extraordinary numbers of men and women turn out for running events staged all over the world. In 1997 the 100th running of the Boston Marathon attracted over 27,000 runners. Running is truly a universal calling.

No sooner does a marathoner recover from one run, than he sets a new goal, establishes a new target and begins again. What is the common bond that draws so many to punish their bodies mercilessly and challenge their wills relentlessly? The runner's true finish line is always set just beyond his reach. Even though he may never attain it, he will always be inspired by it.

It's not the material rewards or the glory that drives runners, although some like to display their growing collection of race T-shirts and medals (with both pride and humour). Motivational experts have proven time and time again that material rewards only inspire us so far. What drives us to succeed is our intrinsic desire to achieve personal goals. It is this desire to strive that makes us human.

What marathon runners do best is establish clearly defined goals and focus meticulously on achieving them within the bounds of reality. However, all runners have a *dream goal.* This goal might always exceed their grasp, but it is what keeps them moving forward.

> "The highest reward for a man's toil is not what he gets for it, but what he becomes by it."
>
> — John Ruskin

"I want to run the Boston Marathon."

Runners also establish interim goals along the way. A typical runner knows where he/she is going for the next year and establishes realistic checkpoints to make sure they are on track. Few marathoners start out as elite athletes. Most begin with modest goals such as, "I want to lose ten pounds." And all marathoners start at the same place – with the first step. Everything that comes after that is focused on building toward the big race and the finish line.

By setting a series of short, medium and long-term goals, runners gradually develop the stamina, techniques and mental attitude that will eventually carry them over the finish line. By starting out too fast or going too far, the runner can end up defeated before he's barely begun, suffering torn muscles, ruined ligaments, a bruised heart and a broken will. As one *Running Room* coach said, "Running fast correlates with absolutely nothing in life."

The ability to set reasonable, measurable goals is the first step in becoming a marathoner in the workplace. Unfortunately for most of us, many of our goals are pre-determined by our employers, our peers or through sheer necessity. These pre-determined goals may be difficult to achieve unless they can be integrated into our personal career goals.

Life will constantly present you with new challenges and exciting opportunities. It's important to ask yourself the following questions on a regular basis so that you will know where you can make changes to your short, medium and long-term goals.

- What would you like to achieve in your career?
- What is the finish line you have set for yourself?
- Are your personal goals and the corporate goals under which you operate compatible?

- Will you become a slave to your career or be made more complete by it?
- Will achieving your career goals fulfill your personal goals?

Striving (or in the running world, "striding") towards someone else's goals will not provide you with the level of motivation you need to succeed. You will lose your conviction, drive and credibility, all of which are essential to the success of your career, especially if you work within the sales environment where belief in yourself is really the only thing you have to sell. If you don't have that spark, that commitment, in your present situation, maybe you should re-evaluate your goals or consider a new career, one where you can see yourself achieving your personal and career goals.

It's important to remember that a goal is unattainable without a vision. You must be able to see your vision clearly and be able to articulate it in a personally meaningful way. It's the vision you see when you look inside yourself, not at the outside world.

Whatever your career, or however long you've been in it, you must constantly re-evaluate your goals and remind yourself of who you are and where you are going. If you are a sales professional, you have chosen a highly competitive arena. Don't be seduced by beating the competition – the only real competitor is you. Your sense of personal pride and achievement will never come from beating someone else, but from exceeding your own limitations and attaining your own personal best.

"Can we not appreciate that our very business in life is not to get ahead of others, but to get ahead of ourselves? To break our own records, to outstrip our yesterdays by our todays, to bear our trials more beautifully than we ever dreamed we could, to give as we have never given, to do our work with more force and a finer finish than ever – this is the true idea: to get ahead of ourselves."

— Thomas S. Monson

• • •

In setting your goals, be realistic about your starting point. The twenty-year-old college track star who sets his marathon sights is starting out from a completely different point than the forty-nine-year-old office worker who is also seeing the marathon as her dream. The college track star may be shooting for victory; for the office worker, crossing the finish line will be the incredible feat. The journey for both requires the same focus, training, determination, and guts.

> I trained for six or eight months and registered for the Ottawa marathon, without the benefit of a coach or discipline of a training program. I was fit, but perhaps not ready mentally for the gruelling distance. I simply didn't know what to expect. I had no idea what race management was all about. The level of fitness I had achieved should have allowed me to run a good marathon. But I simply had no idea how to do it.

I can remember starting out, ignorant of the challenges that would come after twenty miles, waving to the crowds and thinking "this is a piece of cake." And off I flew through the first half at a six-minute pace that was way to fast for me. I can remember being just a mile or so beyond the turn-around point, seeing the other guys in my group across the canal, and I remember waving and thinking "life is good" as I continued my dash to the end. But at the twenty-mile mark, as I started climbing the hill up to the Parliament Buildings, I began to realize that life wasn't that good; I had run out of steam. I didn't know if I had six miles left in me, but I sure wasn't going to quit then. So I walked, waddled and stumbled on for the final six miles. The guys I had passed earlier passed me at their more sensible pace. It was the tortoise and the hare all over again. And I staggered across the finish line of my first marathon.

I would continue to run my next five or six marathons in this manner, charging out full steam for the first twelve, fifteen, seventeen miles and then running out of steam, hitting the proverbial wall. My racing would become more successful as I gained maturity and began to understand the concepts of training discipline, race strategy and pacing. But coming out of that first race, I did set a goal. I wanted to run a sub 3 1/2 hour marathon, which I would go on to accomplish in 1989.

If you're just starting out in a career as a financial professional, your goals will probably be different than those of a seasoned advisor, even though you both may share a similar dream goal of being financially independent and professionally recognized by your peers by the time you're fifty.

As you establish your short, medium and long-term goals, remain realistic about your targets. Make the goals challenging, but make them achievable. Don't expect to immediately achieve what others in the field have spent a lifetime developing. It is important to keep in mind that you have to set goals that are a little outside your comfort zone. You need to force yourself to stretch and reach so that you are continually challenging yourself.

Your goals should be expressed in both qualitative and quantitative terms – the more tangible and measurable your targets are, the easier it will be to evaluate your progress. For example, you may state that your goal is to become recognized as the estate-planning expert in your community. To achieve such a goal you need to break it down into measurable steps. It might look like this:

- Set a five-year goal to build an asset base of 50 million dollars comprised of a client base of 500 families.
- Each family would have a minimum account size of $100,000.
- Establish reasonable targets for this year, the next six months, even for this month. Remember to set your targets so that you are challenging your limitations – reaching beyond your comfort zone.

I suggest that a person new to the business adopt the same strategy I do when I'm planning a training program for a marathon. That is, keep the vision of the long-term goal in mind – the 50 million dollars over five years – but break your goals down into weekly, monthly, quarterly, half and yearly goals. By looking at your goals weekly, you will get an up-to-date review of where you are in the progression to your five-year goal. Again, look at my running plan: I review my training progress weekly, look at the number of miles or cross-training I have done and make adjustments accordingly. By starting off with a weekly review, you make the needed adjustments on an ongoing basis.

Then I do a monthly review to see the status of my plan. My short-term target may have been to run 60 miles a week for the first month. Did I achieve it? If I did, should I carry it through for another month? Your target may have been to have a million dollars in assets the first month. How close were you? Or did you surpass that first month's target? This progressive pattern allows you to stay current or in touch with your long-term goal by breaking it down into smaller, manageable targets.

But the key to any plan, short-term or long, is that you must commit to putting it in writing. You cannot accurately monitor a long-term goal if you don't put it on paper. It is the only way to visually track where you are going. For years I had a calendar blotter on my desk and I would write my miles and my sales on it daily and then transfer that information to my weekly diary. It doesn't have to be long and detailed, but it has to be on paper.

A successful runner recognizes and respects his limitations, yet continues to develop strategies to push those limits a little more each time he hits the pavement until they are no longer a hindrance to obtaining the long-term goal. This is what training is all about both in our personal and professional lives.

Train like the runner and assess your current strengths and limitations. No matter what stands between you and your goals, establish a strategic training schedule that will allow your strengths to carry you towards achieving those goals.

An old Chinese proverb suggests that the only thing worse than not achieving your goals is achieving them; we must always have something to strive for. You must be realistic about setting your goals, with the exception of the "dream goal." We always need the dream!

Chapter review:

1. Determine your "Dream Goal"
2. Break down your dream into smaller, achievable goals
3. Commit them to paper
4. Keep them in front of you always
5. Review them regularly

The appeal of the marathon lies in the clarity of the goal. I found that much of what I learned as a runner could be used in the business world. It was simple things, like picking a race. How do I select one? Do I pick it because of location or distance or prestige or do I simply find it by accident? What distance do I want?

When you decide to run a marathon and select a race, you have a clear understanding of the goal. You can define this goal in a highly tangible way: "I am going to run 26 miles on November 3rd in under 4 hours." You also know what you must do in order to be prepared to step up to the starting line. You understand the discipline it will require. You also know that it will make great demands on your body, mind and spirit and there is no possibility of "faking it." The hours pounding the road, the solitude in running alone, the fatigue, pain and sweat are all very real. But the vision of that finish line, those last hundred yards, keeps you focused, the motivation coming from within.

CHAPTER TWO

Setting Out

"Running is simple! Put one foot in front of the other, quickly repeat, keep going." — Mark Remy

A journey of a thousand miles begins with a single step. From that step onward your journey will be uniquely yours. Like the marathon hopeful, your efforts will be directed towards your ultimate dream goals in a disciplined and focused manner.

Before establishing a personal training program, a runner must first assess his or her level of fitness, athletic ability and any other factors that might affect their training. It's not until you understand your limitations and strengths, and the setting in which the training must take place, that your journey can begin.

In your professional career a good place to start is to ask yourself the following questions:

- Why do you think you will be successful in this highly competitive profession you've chosen?
- What can you offer your clients, the industry and yourself that differentiates you from the

thousands of others who step up to the starting line?
- What is your educational background?
- What kind of professional credentials do you hold?
- What personal qualifications do you have?
- How do your personal life and outside interests contribute to the person you are?
- What other commitments shape your life?

The successful financial advisor builds his portfolio from a solid appreciation of his current reality, understanding that there is no such thing as instant gratification.

•••

Competing in the financial arena is like running the Boston Marathon – there are so many sleek, trained and pumped-up bodies that the runners have to launch themselves from the starting line in groups – over a four-hour period!

Gone are the days when all you had to do was sell a product and close a deal. Today you are not only selling a product, you are selling a *relationship*.

Relationship selling is more than just a trendy phrase that gets bandied about in sales seminars; it's a philosophy that is rooted in the connection that you develop with each and every one of your clients. But this buyer/seller, client/advisor relationship starts within the seller himself. As a salesperson, you first have to build a positive relationship with yourself before attempting to do the same with others.

Before you can promote yourself, you must know who you are. To know who you are – your limitations and strengths and what training is required – you'll need to complete a personal assessment.

In determining your career path you have to ask yourself if you are "manageable." What type of personality do you have and how does that relate to where you want to go? I spent many years in the banking business, starting out as a teller and working my way through the ranks to branch manager, serving in that role in several financial institutions. I eventually came to the conclusion that it wasn't really where I wanted to be because I didn't take direction well or perform well within the constraints of a bureaucratic environment. I needed more freedom. I needed an entrepreneurial environment that would allow me to establish my goals and pursue my plans more independently. I needed a career path that would be more analogous to my-long distance running. So I changed my career path and chose a financial planning role, because it gave me the opportunity to be on my own, determine my own goals, establish my plans, structure my time in a manner that more closely resembled my running discipline. I needed a work environment where my efforts and results were more closely linked and where I could be more dependent on myself.

Personal Assessment

The outcome of completing a personal assessment will be your first step toward achieving your dream goal. As mentioned at the beginning of this chapter, the runner needs to know exactly his strengths, his weaknesses and determine other factors that could play a significant roll in his training program. You as a professional must do the same before you can plan your strategy to enter into the career of your choice.

Your personal assessment should begin with detailing your education, past employment and other interests. This should focus on all accomplishments in every area of your life. By going back and reviewing what you have achieved in the past, and by being honest with yourself, you'll begin to appreciate your strengths and accomplishments both professionally and personally. Becoming more aware of your previous achievements will help give you the self-confidence you'll need to stride towards bigger and more challenging goals. It will also help you recognize the limitations that proper training will help you conquer.

Once you have completed your personal assessment you will know if you are prepared to reach the next target.

Professional and Educational Qualifications

Today, like most professions, the financial industry demands a high level of education and professionalism from its members. If you're just entering this field, a certain level of educational and professional proficiency, and in some cases, specific licensing, will be required before you can step up to the starting line.

You must be willing to invest in yourself whatever you need to succeed. Don't skimp on knowledge – it could result in disaster later.

> I remember a few years ago, after training long hours for a marathon, I decided at the last minute to buy myself a new pair of "econo" running shoes. They held up fine until about the halfway mark, when they suddenly went flat and I felt like I was running in bare feet. That decision to save a few dollars up front cost me the race in the long run. Your willingness to invest in yourself throughout your journey will ensure that you never get caught with "bare feet."

Sometimes in order to cross the finish line faster, you have to risk not crossing it at all. A runner becomes very good at pacing himself to finish, but that creates new limitations. To get across in under that elusive mark, you have to push for the necessary pace from the very beginning, even if it means that you may not finish at all. Risking failure, risking being hurt, is what's so hard to do ... and not just in running!

•••

Product Knowledge

Although I stated earlier in this chapter that you're in the business of relationship selling, it doesn't excuse you from knowing the products that are your tools. Practical knowledge of your products will increase your confidence level and give you more credibility in building your professional relationships. You won't need to sell these tools, because your client will feel confident in your ability to utilize these tools appropriately on his behalf.

In order to continually improve your performance you must always be learning. Practical knowledge can be acquired both in a hands-on manner and from other professionals and mentors in your profession. You need to learn everything you can about your products and how they stack up against the competition. You can't afford to get caught with out-of-date or inaccurate information. If you don't know something, admit it and then get the answer.

Appearances Count

We often place too much emphasis on the superficial stuff, designer labels, BMWs, fancy laptops, sumptuous offices – the accoutrements of success. But appearances do create a certain level of comfort for the client and confidence for the professional.

Stand back for a minute and take a good look at yourself and your surroundings. Now put yourself in the shoes of a prospective client. Go through the following checklist:

- Does your office project a feeling of pride and success?
- Does your office portray quality and efficiency?
- Are all visible tools/products organized and easily accessible?
- Do you inspire confidence?
- Does your appearance complement your profession?

When you look in the mirror what do you see? You need to ensure that your outward image promotes self-confidence. Your physical appearance and well-being should reflect the inner strength and determination that foster your success.

Endurance is the name of the game in long-distance running and in your career. A successful marathoner never enters a race without being in prime shape. The demands are too great. Like a runner, the career demands you make on yourself will require that you have confidence in your physical condition.

Whether the demand is physical, mental or emotional, enormous energy is required, not just in short-term bursts but mile after mile, sale after sale, and client after client.

You are asking your client to trust you, often with his life's savings. First impressions count. Your appearance should validate this trust.

A Final Check

Your assessment of your formal education, professional qualifications, product knowledge and your personal presentation will define your starting point and determine your training needs. In each of the following chapters I will present training concepts that will teach you how to continually push back your limitations as you stride towards your goals.

Determination, discipline and a winning attitude are crucial in achieving goals no matter how big or how small.

Once a goal is chosen, you must create an environment and make those detail choices that contribute to a successful outcome. Too often we take what is offered rather than being selective in our choices. As a runner, I learned to attend to the smallest details. For example, I will try on fifteen, eighteen pairs of running shoes before I find a pair that fits and feels comfortable. I'll be running 600 miles in those shoes; anything less than a perfect fit will hinder my progress.

How much time do we spend checking out our "equipment" before we begin a business journey?

The appearance that is important is the one that builds confidence—not merely impresses.

•••

Running, like any other sport, has not escaped the invasion of designer label frenzy. The seasoned runner simply runs in what's comfortable. But the novice may feel a little more like a runner if attired in properly coordinated running wear. If giving the "appearance" of being a runner helps one "feel" more like a runner, then the investment is worthwhile. The sportswear manufacturers understand that they are not in the business of selling fashion, they are in the business of selling confidence in one's athletic ability. A recent Saucony (running shoes) advertisement simply stated, "Confidence is knowing that there can always be two more miles."

Chapter review:

- Perform a personal assessment. The result will be a resume that you are proud of, one that will build your self-confidence.
- Determine your qualifications. Do you have what it takes and what is needed to pursue your career? Are you qualified for your chosen profession? Do you require additional education or licensing? What can you do to further yourself?
- Learn everything you can about what you are selling. Knowledge builds confidence, which builds relationships.
- Appearance is important; first impressions count. You and your environment should project a confident, warm and welcoming atmosphere to others.

Proper coaching can help you gain confidence more quickly by ensuring that your training and energies are focused on the results you want to achieve. Sometimes this means doing things that you don't enjoy. As a long-distance runner, I am most happy running long distances. But if the only thing I do each week is run a hundred miles at a comfortable pace, I will never achieve my maximum performance in a marathon. To do that I need to incorporate strength training, speed-work, hill-work and appropriate cross-training. I don't like running up and down hills – it's not fun! But I know it will make me a better distance runner. A coach keeps you focused on doing those things that will ultimately help you achieve your goals.

CHAPTER THREE

Coaching
Mentoring and Brief Encounters

> "No one makes it on their own. Everyone who has ever done a kind deed for us, or spoken one word of encouragement to us, has entered into the make up of our character and of our thoughts, as well as our success."
> — Unknown

Long distance running is a solitary discipline, and although a marathoner must run his race alone, many have accompanied him on his journey. Some are by his side for much of the way; others touch him briefly but inspire him greatly.

Some people can remain at a distance but have a lasting impact on who we become. The people who change us, influence us the most, are those who help us discover faith in ourselves and the courage to reach beyond our limits. When we reach a finish line or achieve our goal, there is a brief moment when we selfishly share the joy with nobody but ourselves. However, in the moments following, we do acknowledge that we didn't run the race alone.

Here are some of the people who are important to us in our journey to the finish line, as well as in our everyday life.

Coaches

Elite runners usually have a professional coach as well as several other specific trainers and support personnel. This group may include a weight-trainer, nutritionist, sports physician, physical therapist and psychologist. These people are responsible for helping the runner stay consistent with his/her purpose and focused on his/her goals.

Coaches don't coddle or give empty praise. Their encouragement is unfailing and their pride heartfelt when goals are attained. They demand constant effort from their students and they enforce a sense of discipline necessary for success.

A coach's role is to help you see yourself more clearly so you can get closer to your goals. There must be the acceptance that life is not a smooth journey; there are obstacles and challenges that must be met. Most people will say they are working hard but effort alone is rarely recognized. It's results that mean something. Just working hard won't necessarily allow you to meet your goals; you've got to understand the process and learn to work effectively towards those goals. That's where coaching can play an important role.

In our business environments we continually have broadly stated performance goals thrust upon us with no real guidelines and support to meet them. Working nine-to-five every day will not guarantee achieving anything but burnout. For goals to be achieved the individual must share them, and the process for reaching them must be clearly defined, the progress consistently monitored.

Today, many individuals are beginning to understand

the value of personal business or life coaches. In order to be successful you must be able to clarify your goals, plan them strategically and evaluate your progress effectively. For most of us this is extremely difficult to do alone. Hiring a personal coach to assist in achieving goals is becoming more popular. The very act of engaging a coach is evidence of your commitment to your goals. It makes them more real, more attainable.

We don't hesitate to hire a golf pro to help us with our swing, or a tutor for our children. Doesn't it makes good sense to seek help from a professional to achieve our dreams?

"Some people come into our lives and quickly go ... Some stay in our lives for awhile, leave footprints on our hearts, and we are never, ever the same." - Unknown

Mentors

A mentor gives us cause for reflection. Unlike a coach who is very active in our life, a mentor plays a more passive role. Often in the background, mentors offer counsel only when asked.

A mentor is a person who helps you look inside yourself. Most professionals who feel successful acknowledge the mentors who have helped them along the way. These individuals are always available to talk and share their experience and wisdom. To be mentored, you must be willing to receive advice and constructive criticism, be willing to listen and be willing to change.

For a marathoner, a mentor need not be a runner. A mentor is someone whose wisdom and understanding help people understand themselves better. A mentor relationship is based on trust.

If ever you are chosen to be a mentor, you should consider it a great honour.

*Coaches believe in you,
mentors have the wisdom you have yet to achieve.*

Training Partners

Most long-distance runners run alone. Some travel with their trusty Walkman; many run at peace with themselves. But most runners enjoy and welcome the occasional company of other runners.

> Not too long ago, I was out West visiting my son Derek and we decided to go for a run with Mark, one of his roommates. The three of us started out at an easy pace, enjoying the day and this rare "guy bonding" moment. Before too long Derek was off like a rabbit leaving both Mark and I far behind. Long easy runs are meant to be enjoyed, not raced, so at the end of the run I mentioned to Derek that if he wanted to keep his running partner he had better not turn their casual runs

into a race. I further explained to him that we all run at different levels and to go out with someone who is just starting off as a runner, or who runs at a much slower pace, and turn the run into a race not only discourages that individual but takes the fun out of the run.

After letting my comments sink in, Derek sheepishly agreed and actually admitted that he had in fact been running most of his casual runs "flat out," not taking time to enjoy the day or the company of his friend and not respecting the needs of his running partner.

How often in a business environment do we see a top producer working with a new recruit, pushing him to a performance level far beyond his current potential? How often do we observe that eager new recruit become discouraged, his confidence and enthusiasm destroyed?

There was nothing wrong with Derek wanting to run fast that evening, he just should have let Mark and me know that he was planning to do a little speed work during our run. In the end, that would have motivated us both. The same holds true for the top producer or achiever. You motivate naturally by the excellence you have achieved, but you must do it within a positive and supportive environment. You first have to enjoy running before you can run fast.

As professionals we need those mutually supportive relationships within our working environment. Working together in an open and trusting manner builds confidence and makes progress more likely.

Brief Encounters

All runners have stories to tell about people who briefly touched their lives, changing them forever. Stories of the human spirit and true courage. And there are also stories of those people whose paths cross ours almost coincidentally who have helped us along the way.

> When Sarah ran her first half-marathon she noticed within the first half-mile a woman a little older than her who had been running beside her from the start. After a few more miles Sarah discovered that Marie was 57 and had run two marathons when she was in her twenties, but had done little running since then. This was her first long run in a very long time.
>
> Both Sarah and Marie agreed to run with each other since their pace was similar; a little mutual support seemed like a good idea. At the 10-mile mark both were beginning to feel some pain and stiffening in their joints, but neither wanted to quit for fear it might prevent the other from finishing.
>
> They persevered for each other, and in so doing discovered strength within themselves. Knowing there was a steep hill at the 12-mile mark, both women slowed their pace and mentally prepared for this final test, relentlessly encouraging each other. They had made a silent pact – both were going to finish.
>
> Together they made it to the top of the hill;

the final half-mile was a downhill slope. Sarah turned to Marie and said, "Girl, we made it! We can roll down the hill the rest of the way!"

They crossed the finish line together. Sarah and Marie probably would have made it across the finish line on their own, but you'll never convince them of that.

Throughout our professional lives we meet people who connect us to possibilities and others who inspire us. The ability to network with those around us, to be open to new opportunities, and our willingness to take risks increase our chances for success. When we confine ourselves to our existing environments and relationships, we eliminate all the possibilities that exist beyond.

Every connection we make has the potential to influence our journey. Nothing is a coincidence.

People come into our lives for a reason, or so it seems.

•••

Friends and Family

In our professional lives we find ourselves not appreciating the support and encouragement that we receive every day from those people closest to us. Family and friends support us unconditionally and we should be thankful. They keep us balanced. We need to make sure that misunderstanding and resentment never enter into these important relationships.

If we include these special people in our vision, allow them to share our passion for the goals we hold, and share in our euphoria when we achieve our dreams, they will continue to encourage us unselfishly.

Remember, family and friends are always watching from the sidelines. They are the ones who matter most.

What I have come to take for granted in myself does have value when shared with others.

...

The Cheering Crowds

Nothing can compare to the emotional strength inspired by the cheering crowds along the final mile of the marathon. There's so little left inside you by that point it's only sheer will that's driving you on. Then you become aware of the noise – the whistling, clapping, yells of encouragement – all from strangers urging you on.

> The 10 Mile Crim Race starts a day or two before when you pick up your race kits and visit the booths and attend various symposiums where you meet some of the elite runners in the word. Being part of this race environment and being caught up in the excitement helps you get your head around

your mission ... you're here to run your best. You need to be part of that race "psyche" to be mentally prepared. There have been races where I have literally walked in right before the gun has gone off, and it just isn't the same. But this time I was there well ahead of time. I was able to get rested, drink plenty of water and get into the race mode.

On the morning of the race, I was up around four or five in the morning and had a bagel and some juice, knowing I needed to have the energy to sustain me through the run. About an hour before the race I started my pre-race routines, stretching, loosening up, running an easy mile to warm up my muscles and focus my mind. About forty-five minutes before the start I did a little speed work to put myself into "sprint mode," because that was how I would run this distance. When I did this race I was running as a "seeded runner," which meant I would be among the first couple of hundred or so starters in a race that attracted more than 8,000 runners. There was a mass of people behind me and I had to be ready to go once that gun sounded. The excitement of that start is overwhelming. More than 25,000 people lined the streets along the start cheering us on. A TSN helicopter flew low overhead capturing the start for the evening news, and just prior to the gun everyone was singing "God Bless America," which really gets you pumped and raring to go. And then you're off.

I remember coming around the corner and over the bridge at the first-mile mark and seeing the big digital clock. At 5:46 I was a little ahead of the race pace I wanted, but the adrenaline had kicked in and I knew I would run well that day. I felt confident; I felt the flow; I was where I wanted to be. It was going to be a good race. I was still running at the front of the pack with the elite runners and it was really a neat experience that I would relive many times again, running on the treadmill in the winter days to come. I settled into my six-minute pace as I approached the hill at the four-mile mark, the TV cameras poised on their rigging to record the runners on their first uphill trek. At the six-mile mark I encountered what the locals referred to as their "mini heartbreak hill," named after the infamous hill at the twenty mile point in the Boston Marathon. With the years of hill training that I'd done, the Crim hill was a piece of cake. But the hill took its toll as more runners fell off and gave in to the climb.

Coming off the hill I then ran through an exclusive area of million-dollar homes. Having run this race before, I knew I would be greeted by people in their designer bathrobes hosing down runners as they strided by. The next stretch was relatively flat and the challenge was to maintain the effort and momentum and not be seduced into relaxing as if on a Sunday run. It's easy to slack off when the terrain doesn't force you to push yourself; you have to keep driving yourself forward.

Coming into the last mile, a local radio station was blaring the kind of music that gives you that crucial surge of adrenaline to carry you to the finish. I've always had a strong finish and put on a final kick to spring down the cobblestone road. Even though there were still dozens of runners around me, as I approached the final chute, hearing the crowds cheering, I knew they were cheering for me, for at that moment it was my race. The satisfaction came in those final few seconds as I crossed the finish line. That's what I'd worked so hard to do. That's what it's all about.

Chapter review:

- Engaging a coach is evidence of your commitment to your goals.
- To be mentored, one must be willing to change.
- Professionals need relationships within their working environments that are mutually supportive.
- Every connection we make has the potential to influence our journey. Nothing is a coincidence.
- In our daily challenges we should remember that family and friends are the ones who matters most.

"We do not believe in ourselves until someone reveals that deep inside us there is something valuable, worth listening to, worthy of our trust, sacred to our touch. Once we believe in ourselves, we can risk curiosity, wonder, spontaneous delight or any experience that reveals the human spirit." — E.E. Cummings

Focus Versus Obsession

There is a huge difference between being focused on a goal and being obsessed with it.

Focus is conscious and self-determined, whereas obsession is unconscious and controlling. Long-distance runners, because of the demands of their sport, must be focused with an intensity – a passion – that verges on obsession but must always be controlled. This passion must never be confused with obsession. One might think that by being so focused, a runner might lose sight of things around him. But by clearly focusing on a goal, a runner gains a sense of acuity that makes him far more aware of his environment and those people and things that surround him. From that awareness he draws strength.

Runners inevitably find others who share their passion and provide mutual support. Competition among peers is what enables runners to achieve their personal best. Continual support and encouragement helps them through the difficult times. Becoming a part of this "runner's world" opens up new doors to opportunities that do more than simply make one a better runner.

The ability to find focus in one's personal or professional life has the same impact on an individual as the marathon goal has on a runner. When you focus on a goal that is so clearly defined that you can almost "touch" it, you become far more aware of all those people and things around you that can help you reach it. As you become clearer in articulating your goals and your values, others begin to understand you better. You might find that those who only casually supported you in the past can now demonstrate their support in more specific and meaningful ways. They get "caught up" in your passion and become excited about participating in your efforts.

If you are in a profession where you must differentiate yourself from others, the task becomes far easier when you can clearly state your goals and your values. People who share those goals and values will naturally be attracted to you, as you will to them. There is a strength that comes from acting from your "core" that propels you towards your goals at a speed you may find astonishing.

CHAPTER FOUR

Training

> "A rocking horse keeps moving, but does not make any progress."
> - Alfred A. Montapert

Achieving your goals requires courage, perseverance and commitment, but the desire to achieve your goals can only come from within.

There are certain "truths" about marathon training that also apply to our professional training. First of all, do not confuse motion with progress. Training must be goal specific. You need to engage in activities that allow you to move toward your goal. If you want to run faster, you must run faster and if you want to run further, you must run further. Training is the process that allows you to strive for peak performance and increase the chances of success. Training is about raising the bar, increasing your efforts, pushing your limitations, and continually putting one foot in front of the other.

Training for your career in the financial industry, or in any career, is about challenging your mind and your character in order to be prepared for the demands that achieving success will make on you. It is about learning how to build the necessary relationships that will allow you to be successful. You need to learn everything about your product and your client that you can. This knowledge increases your ability to succeed.

In training, one "Start(s) by doing what's necessary, then what's possible and suddenly you are doing the impossible!"
- St. Francis of Assisi.

Training Begins With Effort

Most of us coast through life living in our comfort zone. We exert precisely the effort needed to accomplish what is necessary and to ensure a modest level of personal success. Sometimes we are inspired to push ourselves a little. Those spurts are sporadic at best but quite often they have surprising results.

A friend of mine was participating in a running clinic to prepare for her first half-marathon. While out running a 3-mile easy run, her group leader asked her, "On a scale from 1 to 10, what effort are you exerting?" She thought for a moment and replied, "Perhaps around 6 or 7 – working hard but not pushing any limits."

In relating this to me a few days later, she told me that she had thought a lot about the concept of effort and its relationship to achieving goals, both in her career and life in general. How did effort fit into the picture? She confessed to me that usually she only operated in the 4 to 6 range, working within her comfort zone and rarely challenging her limits. "Maybe that's why I never feel any great sense of pride or accomplishment. I simply do what I have to do to get the results I'm expected to achieve. What I do comes more from habit than will."

Unless we are willing to push beyond our limitations, and reach for goals outside our grasp, there can be little satisfaction. We know that goals are transitory; once reached, the line gets pushed further ahead. Increasing the effort made and pushing beyond one's limitations is what's exhilarating. It's only through exertion that we raise our own bars.

Upon realizing this, my friend wistfully imagined what she might have accomplished had she applied more effort in the past. Looking back, however, never allows you to move forward. Your focus must always be on the path up ahead. By purposely increasing your effort far beyond your comfort zone even for short periods of time, you will raise your bar.

"If running marathons were easy, everybody would be doing it, but they're not.... You've got to be committed to your training. If you're not focused on success, you won't be successful. You'll never succeed if you're not willing to prepare." -Bill Wenmark, Coach

•••

I remember one year when I was running the Crim Road Race. Although I wasn't in the lead pack, I was close enough to see the motorcycle that was leading the group take a wrong turn, with its flock dutifully following. The lead runners ran about a quarter of a mile down the wrong street before they realized the mistake. Instead of panicking, they simply turned around and ran back up the street, the whole time staying focused on their goals and the challenge that lay ahead. Had they chosen to dwell on the mistake of the motorcycle, chances are they would not have gone on to complete or win the race. The extra effort that was needed to put them back in the lead, showed why they deserved to be on the winner's podium.

Discipline and Schedules

One of the greatest challenges faced by any self-employed professional is the absence of an imposed working structure. With no one to tell you what your working hours are, what your responsibilities entail, what your targets and strategies should be, your ability to impose self-discipline will determine your success.

> The disciplines we employ as athletes can and should be used in our daily lives. My running has greatly influenced me professionally and personally. Each mile brings you closer to your goal. When racing, or just running, you never look

back; it's what's up ahead that's important. The same holds true in your workplace. Although you may learn from what has occurred in the past, you must always be focused on where you are going. The journey is never constant but always changing, and you must have the patience, flexibility and discipline to cope with the changes, as well as having a plan with clear goals and direction. If you don't have that, you are going to flounder and never achieve what you desire.

I began using some of the discipline learned in running in my professional life almost without knowing it. I had entered into a high-pressure position with constant performance challenges. But I was able to catapult my goal-setting and training experiences as a runner into my career and the results have proven to be very successful.

I began by asking myself what made top athletes successful. At the same time I had opportunities to travel extensively worldwide and listen to some of the top business people share their experiences and successes. Both Buck Rogers and Michael Eisner were long-distance runners who used the discipline found in running as a tool to achieve success in their careers. I started to see the correlation between what I was doing as an athlete and what I was trying to do as a businessperson. The more I applied in the workplace the disciplines discovered while running, the more successful I became.

Getting Started

Marathoners work with training schedules as they build toward the big race, establishing, attaining and surpassing increasingly demanding milestones. In addition, any runner planning for a marathon can tell you months in advance the specifics of his training schedule. That schedule is written down in detail: what days of each week he'll run, how long each run will be, the purpose and intensity of each training session, and interim races scheduled along the way with target times already in place.

A written plan does not ensure success, but it does help you focus on your goals and make adjustments along the way. It is also rewarding to look back over the years and reflect on all that you have accomplished.

A new runner recently remarked that within six months she had increased her performance four times over her first race. She ran her first 3-mile in August and six months later ran her first half-marathon.

"Just imagine," she said, "if I had applied the same desire and discipline to my profession that I did to my running over the past six months, my growth in performance would have been extraordinary!" The possibility of running a half-marathon race, for her, had not even been a dream; it had been an impossibility. However, with effort, training and discipline, inspired by desire, she began to do what was necessary, then what was possible, until she found herself doing the impossible.

Your own training schedule as a financial professional requires goal-setting targets and strategies that you need to commit to paper, review regularly and constantly keep in front of you to stay motivated and on target. Be very specific about scheduling activities that produce results. Those activities will most likely involve interaction with your clients. Do not allow any other activities to interfere on those designated training days.

You should not expect to train hard every day. Two good workouts each week is a good goal. The other training days can be less intense, but they are also critical to reaching your goals. Your schedule needs to include activities that build confidence, and interactive activities that give you an opportunity to increase product knowledge and improve your presentation skills.

Plan your schedule so that you can maintain your focus and discipline with enough flexibility to accommodate unforeseen events and other obstacles. Careful preparation is the only path to success.

"....winners and losers are both self-determined, however only winners will agree."   -*Running Times*, Feb. 2000

...

Flow

Flow is the coming together of challenge and skill so the outcome is a sense of rhythm, strength, naturalness and well-being. Flow is what's behind the "runner's high" and what propels the runner towards his or her goals. It is achieved when one's ability and the challenge undertaken are "in sync."

If we tackle a challenge for which we are unprepared and lack the required skills, the result will be frustration and possibly defeat. If you are unprepared to see your client or run your seminar, the outcome you desire will not be achieved. You will not present the competence and confidence required for them to believe in you.

On the other hand, if we take on a challenge we are overly qualified to meet, the outcome is boredom and mediocrity. Sometimes the most mindless tasks are the most difficult to accomplish, and understandably so. If there isn't a challenge there isn't a flow. You'll be amazed at the feeling you will experience when you discover the flow – the feeling that increases one's self-belief and inspires one to even greater feats.

The Loneliness of the Long-distance Runner

The path towards any personal goal can be lonely. How you pursue your goals is unique to you. Your training and scheduling must reflect your individual goals and starting point. They must also reflect the reality of your situation. Goals can sometimes take over, causing you to charge relentlessly towards a finish line that has already become obsolete.

> Recently I was talking to a manager who had just completed her performance review. She was sharing some of the discussions that had transpired during that meeting. When asked by her boss what her development goals were for the year, this manager mentioned she was planning to take a

course in computer training. When asked why, her reply had been that she didn't really want to take the course, but felt she should since she wasn't "very good with computers." Her boss then asked her what she felt she was good at? Without hesitation she had responded, "I really like the human relations part of my job and I am good at that." It was her boss's reply that surprised me. She asked, "Then why don't you take a course in something you are good at and get better at it?"

Why not indeed? How often over the years have we taken courses that we really didn't have an interest in simply because we thought we should take them or, in some cases, were required to take them. At least in the latter situation it's a means to an end. But when we have a choice, why would we want to spend time and energy trying to get a bit better at something we do poorly, with the best possible outcome being mediocrity? How often have we as parents, managers or even friends suggested to someone that they should take a course that we consider useful, without really looking at their strengths and personal goals. Too often we dwell on a person's weaknesses rather than helping them take their natural talents and strengths to the next level.

Don't allow yourself to become a slave to your goals. Goals serve only to provide you with a vision that keeps you inspired.

Staying Loose, Staying Limber

In your professional environment markets can change rapidly, new players suddenly appear on the scene and the economy can take an unexpected nosedive. By adopting a marathon runner's credo of "staying loose and staying limber" you can quickly adapt to changing environments. When circumstances alter you must be ready to change your pace or direction. Your role as an advisor will also change with market conditions and client needs. At times you will be a seller, at times a teacher, at other times a coach and, sometimes, a good listener. Your sensitivity and willingness to adapt to change are critical to your success.

"Rest is as important as running. It allows me to push forward, renewed and ready for the challenge. I listen to my body. If it tells me not to run, I rest. I also listen to my spirit. It needs the boost I get from running. My spirit is renewed when my feet carry me forward into the wind."

- Dolores E. Cross, from Breaking Through the Wall

The Importance of Rest

Somewhere along the way our work ethic eliminated rest. Rest was for the indolent. But the quest for incessant production results only in mediocrity. Peak performance demands rest. Enlightened business and personal coaches recognize the importance of rest in achieving goals, but find that this is one of the most difficult components to instill in an individual's "training program."

Elite runners respect the need for rest; some do it reluctantly but know their performance will greatly suffer without it. For most of us, free time is something we view with guilt. Ignoring the need to renew our energy and nourish our souls causes fatigue, stress and ultimately burnout. A little more rest and perhaps a lot more laughter would go a long way towards improving performance and achieving greater success.

> As an athlete I learned the necessity of warming up and stretching before demanding performance from myself. I'm not suggesting that everyone has to do aerobics in the morning, but if you arrive at the office full of tension, stressed out from the morning commute, shoulders cramped and mind distracted, your performance will be diminished despite the effort made.
>
> I travel a great deal in my profession, and dealing with the fatigue and physical stress caused by travelling is crucial. As a runner, fatigue and stress can impact performance perhaps more than anything else. As business people we often ignore

that. One of my greatest concerns, both for my personal and professional well-being and that of my peers, is the tremendous amount of pressure people are put under to achieve in an increasingly competitive environment. The relentless pressure to outperform oneself, one's peers and the guys on the street drives us towards exhaustion. Running has taught me that we have to learn to pace ourselves.

A career is not a sprint. Our careers are a distance run and all the elements that contribute to marathon success can be used in the workplace. There must be a healthy balance between pushing yourself and pacing yourself.

Chapter review:

- Training requires effort. This means stepping outside of our comfort zone.
- Without discipline and schedules, training cannot work properly.
- Your training is as unique as you are. It is designed to reflect your goals.
- Be adaptable. Environments change, needs change. Be flexible.
- Respect the need for rest.

Building confidence is rarely an uninterrupted linear or upward progression. Life's obstacles challenge our self-confidence as they force us to reconsider our goals. In my case, cancer forced me to change some of my athletic goals. But in changing my goals, I had to regain my confidence. I was no longer able to achieve my previous performance levels for physical reasons. I was growing older and work demands made it impossible. I had to accept those limitations and establish new goals and objectives that continued to challenge me, but in different ways. I had to accept the fact that what I desired when I was thirty was quite different than what was important to me now.

My confidence returned as I understood more clearly the changes that had occurred in me. What I realize now is that I might have reached this understanding much sooner with the support of a coach who could have helped me be realistic and yet still focused on my goals.

Work goals change as well during one's career. What motivates a more mature wholesaler in the financial service business is far different than what motivates a twenty-eight year old "hotshot." My confidence today is no longer derived solely from performance but from experience and competencies gained over time.

CHAPTER FIVE

Challenges

"Success is not measured by the position one has reached in life, rather by the obstacles overcome while trying to succeed."
— Booker T. Washington

"Hitting the wall" is an experience all long-distance runners face. This wall symbolizes the moments in life when all our physical and emotional energy is depleted. When it feels like there's nothing left.

The runner experiences it somewhere between the eighteen- and twenty-three-mile mark. It is as real as any brick wall and the runner hits it with a force and finality that makes going any further seem impossible.

Few runners quit after hitting the wall. Their goal is to finish the race, not merely start it. And, even though in that moment a runner swears never to run another marathon, he knows that he will. The wall is just another obstacle. Every time he hits one he will know how to conquer it the next time.

In our personal and career lives the "walls" we face are the same as the runner's. They are obstacles that impede our progress and make achieving our goals appear impossible. A runner hits the wall when his body physically breaks down. The walls we hit in our professional life are more complex.

I remember the first seminar I had to do standing up in front of a roomful of people to deliver a PowerPoint presentation. I was scared to death. Now, after having given so many presentations it's become second nature, no longer the formidable task it once was. Confidence grows as a function of your training, experience, practice and successes.

My running has broadened my own understanding of my own capabilities and changed how I view my limitations.

...

Events and circumstances beyond our control create many of these walls. Economic downturns, mergers and acquisitions, volatile markets, increased competition, the fickleness of the consuming public, and changes in the regulatory environment can have a major impact on our ability to reach our goals. The results of hitting these walls – financial stress, interpersonal conflict, change in status, displacement, failure to meet production criteria, loss of market share – contribute to our "perceived failure." And our perceived failures make conquering the obstacles seem even more difficult.

There are also walls we create within ourselves

through stress, emotional upheaval, mistrust, isolation, fear and laziness. Regardless of how the walls are built, the results are the same.

We may experience a loss of self-confidence, lack of motivation, a failing belief in our ability to achieve predetermined goals, a growing sense of victimization, and an increasing desire to give up because we think the goal is no longer possible. Where there once was a vision of success, we now see failure. We need to find a way to tackle the wall so that we do not withdraw from those around us or retreat into depression.

How we overcome the walls in our careers depends very much on the type of wall we're facing. We have three choices: We can turn back, we can go around it or we can go over the wall.

Let's look at the walls that force us to turn back. With these walls, we find ourselves in a situation where we can't conceive of a solution and can't even muster the strength to try. Turning back may seem the easiest route to take – especially when well-meaning, sympathetic people tell us that "giving up" is okay. There are, of course, those times when conceding defeat may seem wisest. But in most cases if we give up, we will always wonder what might have been if we had only tried.

What about the walls that demand we go around them? Walls that make us look for a new direction when the path becomes impassable. They are usually created by external circumstances beyond our control. These walls demand we find the courage to overcome some of our fears. Fears that we might have about learning new skills, taking on new challenges, and redefining our goals. Our goal or purpose has not been challenged, only the route we were following. These unexpected detours will usually change our life. If we view them in a positive light, they are not walls, but new opportunities.

Next are the walls that must be scaled. Climbing over these walls demands the most courage, effort and sense of purpose. Failure may seem likely, but not trying will be more devastating. Some people work best when faced with a crisis. Their true passion comes through; their commitment to their vision never wavers – it is always clearly in front of them.

Holding onto the vision you began with is what keeps you from quitting. When you finally manage to overcome the obstacles, you are stronger because you know that you did it – you achieved your goal.

We learn the best lessons from our failures and hard times. We reveal the most about our true character when faced with difficulties and challenges. What we learn from these experiences is that we *can* go on. This is valuable information for anyone who chooses to push his or her limits.

> During a race, a runner must confront his wall alone. The loneliness of the long-distance runner is epitomized in the image of a runner grimacing as he struggles to get beyond the wall.

...

In our day-to-day life it is not necessary to struggle alone with our walls. We can seek the support of friends, peers, coaches and other professionals who can help get us through the hard times.

Motivational programs and speakers, specific skill training programs and individual mentoring, accompanied by a healthy sense of humour, can make life a lot easier. Too often we see it as a sign of weakness to seek help. It isn't. It's a sign of strength to know when to turn to others for help. Just remember that when you do seek help, it's important to go to those who will urge you to keep trying.

> Not long ago I was coaching a friend to her first marathon. Jinny had been buoyed by the many personal bests she had achieved along the way in

shorter course races and had steadily improved her performance over the half-marathon as well.

About a month before her marathon debut, Jinny entered another half-marathon. Her expectation was that she would achieve another personal best, possibly break the two-hour mark and feel confident about her prospects in the upcoming marathon.

It was a warm fall day. Jinny hadn't properly anticipated the impact the heat might have on her. She ran the first half of the race well. She was on target for another personal best. But around the seven-mile point she encountered "the wall" for the first time. Her heart and lungs felt like exploding, her legs felt like lead, her body ached and her focus vanished. She reached deep inside but couldn't find anything in reserve. She felt like quitting. But quitting wasn't an option.

Jinny found it almost impossible to go on. She forced herself to start moving again, one foot in front of the other. Her only motivation now was to finish the race in what would be her worst time – a difficult goal to pursue. Somehow she made it to the finish. Jinny came out of the experience totally defeated. "How can I ever run a marathon if I can't even do a half? I was a fool to think I could do it." She immediately doubted herself, because she wasn't able to recognize her newfound strength.

This was one of those teachable moments, when a coach does not offer pity but holds up a mirror. "You told me you hit the wall at seven miles," I said.

"That's right."

"You also told me you finished the race, right?"

"Well," she confessed, "I crossed the finish line ... barely."

"So even though you had nothing left," I said, "you found enough inside you to do nearly six more miles. You didn't quit. That will be very important to remember when you hit the twenty-mile point in your marathon."

"Perhaps having a 'good race' is a race where you mentally conquer your walls, big and small".

•••

Walls are created to help us discover the strength and courage we never knew we had. Winning is more about not quitting than anything else.

People who are successful in their careers or personal endeavours have rarely found the road smooth. Most share their stories about their personal failures, the obstacles and tragedies that nearly destroyed their vision and their goals. Worthwhile goals cannot be achieved if you are not prepared to risk defeat. Don't set out on your journey if all you desire is a "safe harbour."

As well as learning how to overcome the walls we will encounter, we also need to make sure we don't create any.

If a runner doesn't pace himself properly, he will inevitably hit the wall. When we don't appreciate our limitations or learn from our experiences we invite walls. In today's working environment we often find ourselves surrounded by walls, many of which are imposed by others, some that are self-imposed.

Experience and self-knowledge are the best guides when meeting such challenges. The "walls" that confront you become your best teachers by validating your vision, fostering true strength and instilling humility.

Chapter review:

- If we don't pace ourselves properly, we will encounter walls.
- Obstacles in our path may be new opportunities.
- Holding firm in our vision can keep us from quitting.
- Our true character is revealed when faced with difficulties.
- Walls are sent to help us discover our strength and courage.

GO THE DISTANCE

"Only those who risk going too far can possibly find out how far they can go." —T.S. Eliot

CHAPTER SIX

The Race

> "If you want to take your mission in life to the next level... if you don't know how to rise, don't look outside yourself. Look inside. Don't let your fears keep you mired in the crowd. Abolish your fears and raise your commitment level to the point of no return, and I guarantee you that the champion within will burst forth to propel you toward victory."
> — Bruce Jenner

Runners run for a lot of different reasons. These may include fitness, a sense of well-being, the simple joy of the movement, and for some, the solitude. Few people choose to run a marathon, not because they do not possess the determination or discipline, but because they do not possess the desire. Runners race because they are compelled to discover just how far they can run.

In the business world, the goal to be self-employed rather than to work for somebody else in a "9 to 5" job is a personal choice, one in which you seek to discover your entrepreneurial capacity. To be self-employed requires the desire to do so. It serves no purpose to pursue a goal just to prove something to yourself or compete with someone else, even though both the proving and competing may provide you with some of the external motivation.

The beauty of the marathon lies in the clarity of its goal and singular ability to test the body, mind and soul. As runners, we race to discover how deep we can reach to find the courage and strength to "go the distance."

A runner steps up to the starting line because he deserves to be there. He has acquired the necessary tools and experience, trained with determination and discipline, and is clearly focused on that vision. The only difference is, now the effort really counts and all the preparation in the world does not guarantee success. Although there may be ten thousand runners surrounding you, the truth is, you're on your own.

"Am I ready?" It's natural to step up to the starting line with some degree of nervousness and even fear. Fear should be a welcome companion since it stimulates the adrenaline that allows you to "do it anyway."

> "The credit belongs to those who are actually in the arena, who strive valiantly; who know the great enthusiasms, the great devotions and spend themselves in a worthy cause; who, at the best, know the triumph of high achievement; and who, at the worst, if they fail, fail while daring greatly, so that their place shall never be with those cold and timid souls who know neither victory nor defeat."
>
> - Theodore Roosevelt

Your determination and desire get you to the starting line. How you manage the race will determine the outcome. In choosing a professional or personal goal with clearly defined outcomes that challenge us beyond our comfort zones, we elevate our day-to-day efforts to new levels.

Before the Race

If at all possible, a runner will tour the course before the race. If he has the chance to train along sections of it, all the better. It's easier to plan your race strategy if you know your course. What are the course elevations like? Are there gentle, rolling hills or the "heartbreak" variety? Is it a scenic route? How frequent are the water stations? Will there be thousands of people at the start? Will pace "rabbits" be there to help keep you on track? When performance is important, you want to avoid surprises.

> I had a wonderful experience running in Thailand. I happened to be going over there for a conference and was reading a magazine on the plane that mentioned that the Southeast Asian Marathon was on during the time I would be there. So I signed up to run it. Although it was an international race, this was only its second year and there were only about fourteen non-Asians competing. The race started at 5:30 a.m. because of the intense heat expected that day. There were throngs of people watching and many came up to me enthusiastically pumping my hand and slap-

ping my back, telling me I was sure to win. Even during the first half of the race, the TV cameras and motorcycles were following me, capturing my progress for later newscasts. I think they had me mixed up with either Eddie Eyestone or Rob DeCostello, because I surely wasn't a contender. But the attention was pretty cool.

The race proved to be very challenging because of the intense heat and poor air quality. There was no pollution control in Bangkok. At the race finish it was probably 120 degrees and maintaining hydration was a real challenge. By the end of the race I had lost fifteen or sixteen pounds of fluid weight just because of the heat. I remember that at the twenty-mile mark someone had set up showers to cool down the runners which I gratefully ran through, little realizing that my soaking wet running shoes would now weigh about four pounds each. I ran the last six miles in heavy, soggy, squishy running shoes ... not a good strategy on my part.

Runners must also be prepared to adapt their planned strategy to actual race-day conditions. The weather conditions and how the runner feels both physically and mentally may dictate last-minute adjustments. The ability to adapt to changing environments is critical to success. As a professional, you need to constantly assess your course and your career. You need to understand the marketplace, your clients and your competition, and you need to know where challenges are most likely to occur. The behaviour of your clients or your competition should never come as a surprise.

Strategy is based on awareness. Professionals should be able to adapt to changes as they occur, shifting gears as easily as runners alter their pace. It is not good enough simply to prepare for important meetings, presentations and decisions. You need to respond appropriately and quickly to the challenges and opportunities that will inevitably arise.

The First Mile and Beyond

A marathon is not a sprint. It requires more than just one short burst of effort. A runner must manage his/her race to maximize the chances for success.

A marathon is run in three stages. In the first stage you run easily, fresh and full of confidence. Your body responds like the well-trained machine it is. The most important thing at this stage is not to be seduced into going out too fast. Because you've been training for so long, holding back will be one of the greatest discipline challenges you'll face, especially when so many other runners around you will explode from the starting line at the sound of the gun. Don't let exuberance be your downfall. Conserve your strength for the finish. Those runners that start out too fast seldom if ever reach the finish.

The same holds true in our business lives. Too many people are "quick-starts" in their new careers. Impressing everyone with their initiative, promises and potential, they rise to the top in the beginning but fade fast, never achieving anything.

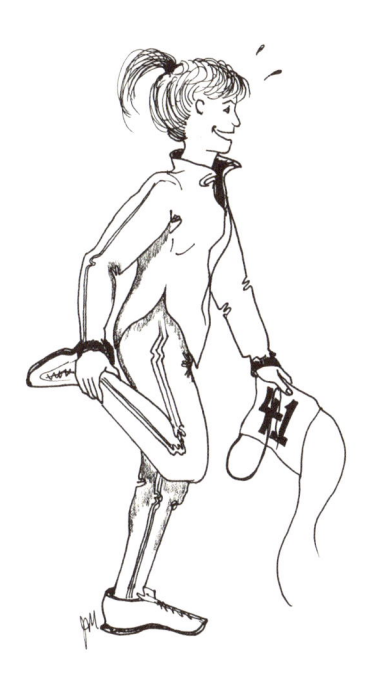

Sometimes you can even avoid the "finish" by changing direction mid-course, so that you will never be called upon to hold yourself accountable to finish what you started. The marathon does not provide the runner with that same luxury. The course is set, the distance measured to an exact twenty-six miles, three hundred and eight-five yards. You either finish or you don't. To run a marathon, race management is critical.

After passing that first milepost, you settle into your race-pace and let your head become your jockey. You know what your planned pace-time is; you even know what that pace feels like. Now you listen to your body.

You must run this race in the present. You run well only if you know yourself. You run confidently knowing that you have trained and prepared properly. You'll make sure you keep yourself well hydrated and nourished along the way. You may include intermittent "rest breaks" to aid recovery and improve performance. Lastly, you may choose to run with a running partner or pace "rabbit" so the journey isn't quite as lonely, but still be "on your own."

In your professional career, self-knowledge and the ability to determine your own pace is also critical. Although you have determined the results you wish to achieve, you need to find a way to manage how you meet your goals.

Stage Two: Reality Time

Near the halfway point of the marathon, reality sets in. You begin to tire a little and yet you still have many miles to go. Knowing that you still have to run as many miles as you've already come can be a bit overwhelming. This is when the heart comes into play. This is when the desire that brought you to the starting line needs to keep you focused and give you strength. You visualize the finish line. You accept the growing fatigue, stiffness and pain as mere companions on the journey. Your management of the race now extends to managing those physical and emotional challenges that reveal the strength of your character and intensify as the miles go by.

In your business or professional life you are constantly confronted with reality checks. What was new and exciting becomes dull and unchallenging. Changes in management can change values and goals. Your clients may become less loyal and the competition more vicious. Market conditions might challenge your confidence in yourself as a professional, and that self-doubt can create a downward spiral. For many it is easier to train to "go faster" than to "go the distance."

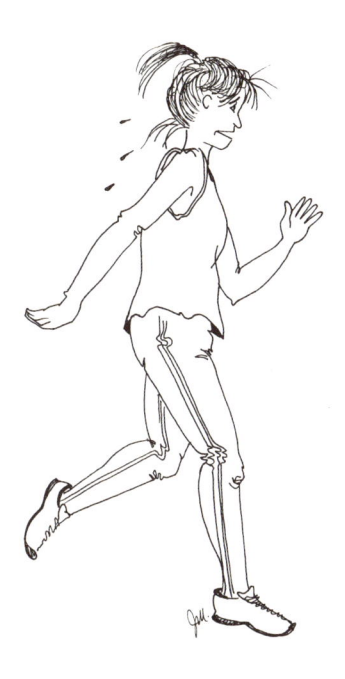

How you manage this part of your career will prove a lot more challenging than managing the "reality check" part of the marathon. In a race, it's just you and the miles. Life, however, is a bit more complicated. You should always strive to know yourself, seek to reveal your character strengths and never lose sight of the goals to which you've committed.

In a marathon, in your career, or for that matter, in your life, it's important that you always run your own race.

Stage Three: Digging Deep...the Final Miles

Somewhere after the eighteen-mile mark, all the rules change. Physically you have nothing left and even the desire is wearing thin. Now there's only one thing that keeps you going and that's the knowledge that you didn't come here to start the race, you came to finish.

How you do it doesn't matter. Some runners "reel in" the runners in front of them; some visualize glorious runs from the past, and some seek energy from the "high fives" and cheering crowds along the route. But all reach deep inside and find the one thing that will get them to the finish – courage.

Perhaps it's the very nature of the marathon that inspires courage. In business, courage lies in meeting performance expectations while maintaining personal integrity.

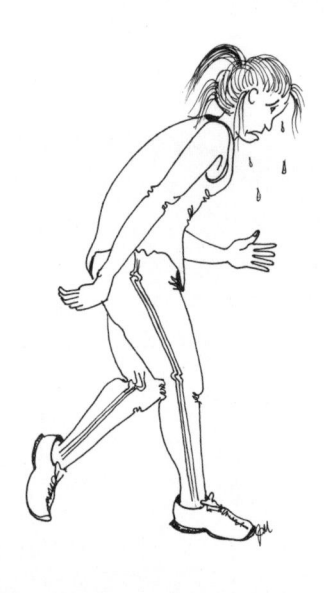

Crossing the Finish Line

Crossing the finish line is an experience unlike any other. It is only a single moment, but it is the sum total of what you have learned from the many lonely miles you ran to prepare for it.

The marathon is truly a thousand-mile journey that begins with a single step. Along the way you learn about the importance of focusing on goals and doing everything necessary to step up to the starting line. Whether running a marathon or pursuing a professional endeavour, no amount of determination or discipline can guarantee success, but without them our goals remain merely unattainable dreams.

Crossing the finish line is easy; achieving your dream goals is easy. It's going the distance that's tough. Believing in yourself, staying focused on your goals and managing your race strategically will help get you to the finish.

Chapter review:

- It serves no purpose to pursue a goal just to prove something or to compete with others.
- To be able to step up to the starting line we must have acquired the necessary tools and experience to get there.
- We must be prepared to adapt to changes in our course, in our careers.
- It's not the distance you have gone that tires you, but the distance that lies ahead.
- Courage in business lies in maintaining personal integrity.

"The last 800 meters were amazing. All of a sudden I felt a surge of energy as realization that I was going to complete my first marathon flooded over me. The crowds were cheering and tears of joy were streaming down my sweat-covered face as I entered the final chute, the finish line in sight. That moment in time will be etched in my memory forever." — First Time Marathoner

CHAPTER SEVEN

The Finish Line

> "Did I win? Have I done enough? Have I been a good enough runner, writer, speaker and doctor? More important, have I been a good enough father, husband and friend? We're doing the best we can with what we have...we're still out here, giving our all. No one can do more or should do less."
>
> - Dr. George Sheehan in his last race

I only enter races where I know I'll get a race T-shirt and better yet, a medal. I like the recognition of my personal accomplishment. In a major race there may be thousands of runners, only a handful of whom may be considered "elite." The rest of the runners are happy to finish, eager to strive for a personal best and hopeful of achieving even better results within their peer group rankings. It's not so much a matter of competing with anyone else than it is the knowledge that you ran the best you could for that race.

In a marathon, "going the distance" deserves recognition. The medal hung around your neck has no intrinsic value; rather it symbolizes the achievement of a personal goal. I

BILL CHAMBERS

2002 Hamilton Around the Bay Road Race

Even when running in a group, long distance runners still run within themselves.

...

display my medals with pride, not arrogance. In each and every race others have always run faster, but I've come away from each knowing I have done my best. My growing collection of race T-shirts and numbers provides further evidence of my racing experiences.

During that same half-marathon in which my friend encountered her wall, there was a very poignant moment at the end of the race that left a lasting impression on everyone.

> A young woman who had recently committed to some very personal fitness goals was running her first half-marathon. For my friend and many others, it had been a difficult race. The heat and humidity affected the performance of even the best-trained runners. The race clock had long ago passed the three-hour mark and all the runners had completed the race except for this one young woman.
>
> As the three-and-a-half-hour mark approached, the race official announced that the final runner was five hundred yards out. No one there needed to be told that their encouragement would help "bring her home." The applause, cheers and tears that accompanied her down that final stretch, and the pride and glowing smile on that young woman's face reminded everyone who watched her what courage was all about. During the awards ceremony that followed, the race official presented a special award to the one who deserved it most.

How unfortunate it is that in our workplace we recognize only the "top" performers. Even more unfortunate is the fact that we have come to define success in quantitative terms. Despite the pretense of professionalism, the competition for such recognition becomes a kind of "sales contest." The players strive to produce more than anyone else, vying for the prize. Some companies even go so far as to report to their sales people on a regular basis, showing "current rankings" and "gross (I use the word in its true meaning) production." Rivalry can become fierce and co-operation non-existent. Such external motivators might produce results, but rarely do they achieve excellence.

Perhaps we need to question whether production or achievement is really the goal? Often the prize is made to overshadow the goal. I'm not suggesting that competition itself is bad. When the competitive spirit is aroused in those striving for a common goal it can be a real stimulant. It can give them an edge or push when they need to maximize their performance.

People tend to play their best game when matched with a player more accomplished than themselves. Competition is healthy when it is used to inspire our best efforts or to raise our level of performance. But too often we find ourselves competing merely for the prize, which we can never win. In not being able to claim the prize, we find it difficult to claim our own victories. So it begs the question, "Why try?"

GO THE DISTANCE

> When racing, or simply running, you never look back; it's what's up ahead that is important.

•••

A prize does not change us. It does not make us a better person. It does not provide value for anybody else. The real reward, the real prize comes from inside ourselves, in knowing that we achieved what we set out to do.

When companies focus only on who is fastest or who produces the most, they fail to recognize the admirable qualities of all the other participants. More importantly, as individuals we fail to recognize our own achievements. It is not always the fastest who is most deserving of our respect. We have come to view respect as a right bestowed by rank rather than a privilege earned by contribution. Such superficial respect never serves to inspire others. It actually undermines the performance of others and fosters jealousy and divisiveness in an organization. Lack of recognition and appreciation does more to destroy enthusiasm and passion than any reward does to instill it.

In our day-to-day life, we all need to make a more conscious effort to recognize the contributions and accomplishments of others. All team members, regardless of their position, deserve recognition. We are more deeply motivated when we feel appreciated by others. That is what makes us truly human.

How often do we feel appreciated in the workplace? How often do we cheer others on? We may be rewarded if we are the best or produce the most, but never for simply doing our best, albeit from a "mid-pack" position. There's no cheering unless you are in the lead in business. But I know how the cheering crowds can inspire performance, and I know that when I've performed my best in the workplace it's been when I've felt most appreciated. We all need recognition for the contribution we are making.

David Novak, CEO of the KFC/Pizza Hut/Taco Bell empire, believes that "recognition drives performance," and by this he does not mean just recognizing the managers of the "best" stores; he regularly recognizes employees in all roles for their efforts in building consumer enthusiasm.

As we learn to appreciate others, especially those who directly support our individual efforts, we will also learn to appreciate ourselves. Appreciation always creates a ripple effect. It radiates outward, touching everyone and everything around us. It creates a positive energy and sense of involvement and commitment that inevitably enhances the performance of the whole team and organization.

Winners never get to the finish line all by themselves. The "high fives" are happening in the pit long after the checkered flag is dropped. As the driver is hoisted onto the shoulders of his teammates, we are reminded that winning is the tangible evidence and recognition of a team driven toward their dream.

Like race T-shirts, gratitude, both given and received, always makes us feel better about ourselves and inspires us towards personal excellence.

We all have our abilities and challenges. We all view our own accomplishments more humbly than those who observe us, because our performance on any given day is exactly the best we can give, nothing more, nothing less.

Chapter review:

- With every finish line, every accomplishment, and every goal achieved, you learn something new about yourself.
- Stay focused on what you will achieve, not on what you will receive when you cross the "finish line."
- Be more conscious of the efforts of others.
- Everyone deserves to be recognized for his or her achievements.
- Gratitude both given and received makes us feel better about ourselves.

People today ask me why I still run after twenty-five years. The answer is simple. I still enjoy it. It's always a challenge competing against your own "best self" and nobody else.

CHAPTER EIGHT

Beyond the Finish Line

"The miracle isn't that I finished. The miracle is that I had the courage to start." — John Bingham

In the final moments of a marathon, you focus on the banner with that wonderful word "FINISH" telling you you're almost there. That banner has been in your vision for the past twenty-six miles and the reality of your accomplishment – your goals – lies just yards ahead. You know that in a few minutes you can finally stop and give your body the relief it has demanded for the last six miles. Mingled with the exhaustion is a euphoria that overwhelms even the most seasoned runner. Finishing a marathon, regardless of the time, is a victory in itself. The euphoria is short-lived because there is a finality to the word "FINISH" that begs the question, "What's next?" We feel empty without goals, and having accomplished one, that feeling of emptiness challenges us to find another.

Rather than thinking of the finish line – or achieving our goal – as an end, perhaps we should think of it as another evaluation point, where we assess what we have achieved in order to determine our next step. For the first-time marathoner, merely completing the race is not only an enormous accomplishment, it teaches the individual much about his capacity to go beyond his limits.

Months after completing my first marathon I experienced a flash of insight into why the marathon had been so significant for me. Up until that point, I had always defined my goals, if I had any, by what I thought were my limitations. In other words, I never would have said that my goal was to run a marathon because I believed that was impossible. But after crossing my first finish line, I realized that I would never again let limitations determine my goals. It should only be our dreams that determine our goals. For me, from that point onward, there were no finish lines, only new beginnings.

When I recognized what I had learned about myself on that first marathon journey, I started to focus more clearly on setting new goals for myself. As well as the joy it brought, the finish line had taught me to recognize the need to eliminate the "walls" that were limiting my progress.

Until recently I'd been looking for those new goals within the context of everything I was currently committed to and limited by. I've come to realize that's not where I'm going to find them. I have been surprised to learn that commitments that were outcomes of earlier goals have themselves become walls. Walls disguised as commitments are not only difficult to discern, but nearly impossible to get over.

Our dreams never come from the question "Why?" Dreams answer the question "Why not?" Perhaps it's only the why not that helps us discover what's beyond the finish line. The finish line is really a transition point where we take a new understanding of our true self and move forward with more confidence. Change, as difficult as it may be, is always a catalyst.

Although many people run only one marathon and hold it as a memory forever, most feel compelled to run again. Running faster, achieving "personal bests" become the goals. "Winning" may be something only the elite can aspire to. But even for the most competitive and most disciplined athlete, going faster soon becomes less important, and with the passing of time, unrealistic.

If going faster were the only thing that inspired the runners that step up to the starting line at a marathon, the numbers would soon dwindle so that only the fastest and the fittest (and the youngest) would persevere. Fortunately, just going faster is not what motivates a runner. The real motivation is a qualitative goal that is measured not in speed but in how you change on the journey. You begin to value the experience as much as the destination; the finish line only symbolizes how "far" you have come.

𝄋

As a runner, you can't expect to run a marathon if you are only prepared to devote the time and effort necessary to run a 10 km race. Your commitment to your business goals is no different.

•••

So, what's beyond the finish line? I pose this question from both a personal and intellectual perspective.

A short while ago, an interesting article was sent to me in which the writer was talking about the difference between "success" and "significance." When we cross a finish line, reach a goal, we feel successful. Success is a sense of personal achievement, a task well done. But beyond that, we achieve a sense of significance.

Significance is the knowledge that we have made a contribution to others or had an impact in somebody's life. Significance carries us beyond ourselves. Success is measured in quantitative terms, but significance is qualitative. Success is soon forgotten; significance lasts forever. If anyone ever remembers us, it's because we've been significant, not merely successful.

Much of our energy is targeted towards future outcomes. Focusing on these goals and dreams may be what motivates us, but we need to remember that taking time to find happiness along the road is what provides us with a sense of fulfillment. Not enjoying the journey is what leads to discouragement and even failure.

When I started running, I chose a destination. I decided that when I could run three miles, I'd be a runner. So I would run, but not make it to the three-mile mark. Day after day I failed to reach my goal. Day after day I accumulated evidence that I was not a runner. The point I was missing about running was the very point I already knew about travelling. The key is to enjoy the journey.

Refusing to feel happy until you reach wherever it is you want to go, or whoever it is you want to be, is the worst possible approach. Waiting to celebrate until the end means missing all the wonderful moments along the way. Every run is a gift; every day is a gift.

Our futures are not preordained, as Bingham so wisely points out. "I have no choice but to enjoy every minute of every run. I'm keenly aware that my destiny lies in every step."

Perhaps then, what lies beyond any finish line is a renewed commitment to finding joy in the present. Inevitably this will allow us to stay more in touch with our values and more purposeful in our journeys.

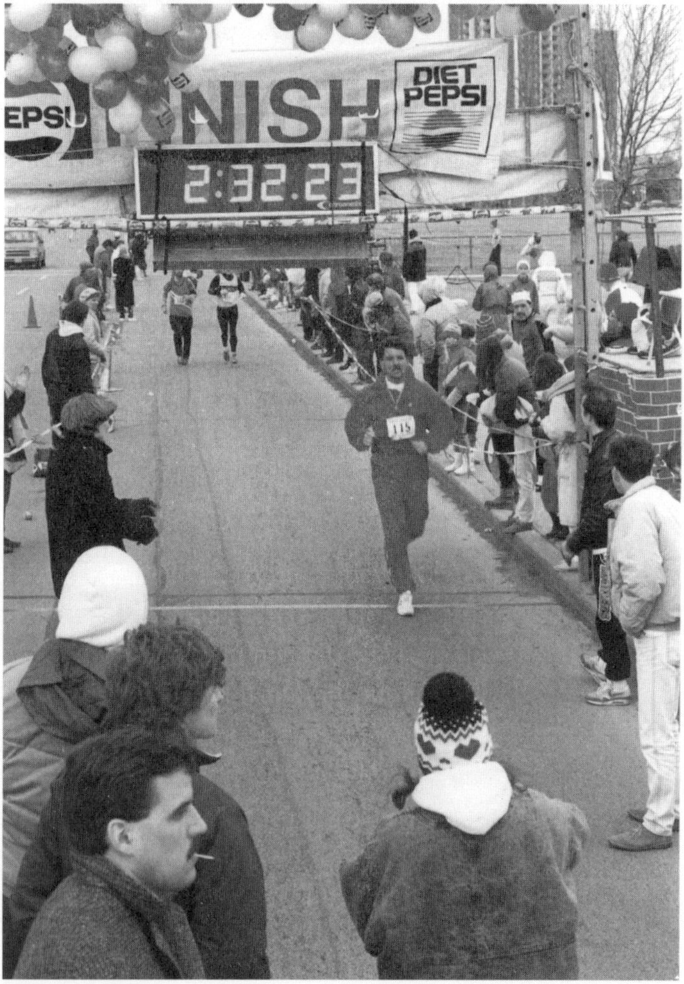
EPSI
NISH
DIET
PEPSI
2:32.23
115

Epilogue

Where does the strength come from to enable you to face the challenges in both your personal and professional life? What's in your "core" that allows you to tackle goals that are difficult? Many of the challenges we face are hard. We risk failure. To take risks you must have passion. When you run into roadblocks you must redirect that passion. Your goals must reflect your desires not someone else's, otherwise you cannot be passionate about achieving them. In your professional life, goals are usually determined by others, making it even more difficult to find that passion. The onus is on you to discover something within that corporate goal that makes it significant for you, that provides the emotional connection.

Where does the sparkle in a runner's eye come from? I know now. It comes from the heart. Running puts a person in touch with their emotions and an incredible source of strength and self-knowledge. That sparkle in their eyes is evidence of the passion in their heart.

So what is the analogy between running and our professional life? I believe it's the search to discover our inner potential, which, once tapped is a source of spirituality, wisdom, compassion and action. When we get in touch with our inner resources, they energize us and give us a sense of meaning and authenticity. We always seem so intent on reaching finish lines and yet, all of us are destined to meet our own inevitable finish line. Perhaps we need to be finding more joy in those precious moments along the way.

And from here ...

I still have fun running and racing. Now when I run through a water station someone inevitably calls out "You're looking good, SIR ... " Either I'm running a whole lot slower or I'm getting old and earning their respect. I don't have to kill myself running a race any more. I can simply enjoy it and still get my reward ... that little medal that says I did it! I keep all my medals and ribbons on plaques. I hold memories of each and every race that have great meaning for me and that I can share with my sons and someday with my grandchildren. My races have been a source of great personal satisfaction.

It has also given me great satisfaction to help someone else become a runner, to coach somebody to their first marathon finish. I had a wonderful experience a couple of years ago when I began coaching Jane, who had agreed to help me write this book. In order to better appreciate running, she decided to try running herself. It was exciting to watch the progress of someone who had never done any distance running as she went from struggling with one mile up and down the hill in front of her house, to running a marathon just a year later.

It was rewarding for me to be coaching her, to appreciate her effort and determination and know the satisfaction she felt in reaching the finish line. It was an enormous challenge for Jane. But she was determined to put the time and effort into the training. I was able to encourage her along the way, sharing my knowledge and experience, giving her strategies to deal with the difficult situations and to help her anticipate what she would encounter along the way. Coaching on the field or in the workplace certainly contributes to success, but the motivation and ultimate satisfaction must always come from within.

In running you don't have other team members to rely on. Once the gun sounds you only have yourself. As Jane's coach it was wonderful to watch her progress as a runner. It was even more rewarding to observe her growing confidence and pride in herself, not only as a runner but as a person. To be a part of that was really special.

I find myself in those positions that wear me down, make me want to quit, but the mental toughness kicks in. I know that I've been there before; I know that I can push through the difficult times, cast aside the self-doubts. I know I can reach the desired outcome. My running has taught me to "GO THE DISTANCE."

— Bill Chambers

WHAT ARE YOUR GOALS?

GOAL #1

Dream Goal: _____

_____

Long-term Goal: (3– years) _____

_____

Medium-term Goal (1 year): _____

_____

Short-term (3–6 months): _____

_____

This month: _____

_____

GOAL #2

Dream Goal: _____

_____

Long-term Goal: (3– years) _____

_____

Medium-term Goal (1 year): _____

_____

Short-term (3–6 months): _____

_____

This month: _____

_____

GOAL #3

Dream Goal: _____
_____

Long-term Goal: (3– years) _____
_____

Medium-term Goal (1 year): _____
_____

Short-term (3–6 months): _____
_____

This month: _____
_____

GOAL #4

Dream Goal: _____
_____

Long-term Goal: (3– years) _____
_____

Medium-term Goal (1 year): _____
_____

Short-term (3–6 months): _____
_____

This month: _____
_____

TAKE A LOOK AT YOURSELF NOW

Personal Inventory

Rate 1 – 5:
(1 – Needs Improvement, 3 – Average, 5 – Excellent)

Personal Image	1	2	3	4	5
Education	1	2	3	4	5
Professional Qualifications	1	2	3	4	5
Health & Fitness	1	2	3	4	5
Product Knowledge	1	2	3	4	5
Office	1	2	3	4	5

What three accomplishments during the past year have increased your confidence?

_____

_____

_____

List five improvement that you wish to make and, for each, show your target date and "to do" for tomorrow.

Improvement	Target Date	"To Do" Tomorrow
1. _____	_____	_____
2. _____	_____	_____
3. _____	_____	_____
4. _____	_____	_____
5. _____	_____	_____

TRAINING LOG

Runners keep detailed training logs of their daily training activities. They use these logs to record time, distances, type of work-out, comments on weather, mood, heart rate, etc. A typical entry might read as follows:

Day	**Distance**	**Time**	**Course**	**Notes**
Oct. 15	5km	28mins	The Lightfoot Trail	Knees a little sore, beautiful fall day Ran at 10km race pace

Use the following example or prepare your own log to keep notes on your daily "training":

Day	**Focus/Purpose**	**Results/Comments**
Oct. 15	Prepare for seminar	Ready! Great PowerPoint presentation (remember to thank Susan)
	Client contact	Called six clients in follow-up to estate planning letter; set up our appointment
	Strategic partners	Set up meeting with new lawyer
	Fun	Went horseback riding

_____   _____   _____

_____   _____   _____

_____   _____   _____

_____   _____   _____

_____   _____   _____

_____   _____   _____

_____   _____   _____

About the Author

When Bill Chambers was nineteen he thought he was invincible. Then he suffered a near-fatal motorcycle accident that forced him to redefine his goals. At twenty-two he began running and over the next twenty-five years ran more than a hundred long-distance races, collecting personal bests and memories that would last a lifetime.

Running helped Bill develop the discipline and strength that have been invaluable in both his personal and professional life. He learned that you don't reach finish lines if you're not willing to start, and the outcome depends on how you decide to approach a situation.

The ability not only to survive, but also to prosper in the new economy, demands a radical new approach because of increasingly sophisticated clients, changing work paradigms and intensified competition.

A financial services salesperson, Bill began to realize that the principles upon which successful marathon running is based have a direct application to achieving goals in our personal life and career – specifically in the sales environment.

Those principles are goal-setting, training, maintaining discipline and focus, and the ability to adapt to an ever-changing environment.

A recent battle with cancer was Bill's second life-altering experience. Once again, running gave him the structure and discipline he needed to regain his strength and find a new focus.

Although not all of us aspire to become marathoners, each of us can benefit from understanding the runner's formula for achieving success. *Go the Distance* shows us how to define our "dream goal," how to redefine our finish lines as starting lines, and how to find the strength to take one more step.

Bill Chambers, lives in Ontario, and is involved in the financial services industry.

We want to hear from you.

Bill Chambers would love to hear how this book has inspired you in your professional or personal life. Please write him with your stories, thoughts and successes that you have experienced as a result of reading this book.

E-mail your stories to:
bill_chambers@canada.com

To order books in quantity or
if you would like to have one sent to a friend,
e-mail us at
bill_chambers@canada.com.

Keynotes and Seminars, Personal Coaching

For more information on how you can book Bill Chambers for your next conference or for personal coaching, email us at:

bill_chambers@canada.com

or call him at

416-690-5275